small
box crafts

Dioramas, Doll Rooms + Toy-Sized Spaces
for Imaginative Play

Publisher: Paul McGahren
Editorial Director: Matthew Teague
Editor: Kerri Grzybicki
Designer: Lindsay Hess
Layout Designer: Jodie Delohery
Illustrator: Carolyn Mosher

Spring House Press
P.O. Box 239
Whites Creek, TN 37189

Paperback ISBN: 978-1-940611-86-0
ePub ISBN: 978-1-940611-99-0

Library of Congress Control Number: 2018966409

Printed in The United States of America

10 9 8 7 6 5 4 3 2 1

Note: The following list contains names that may be used in *Small Box Crafts* and may be registered with the United States Copyright Office: Apple (iPhone); DC Comics (Batman); MARVEL (Spider-Man); and Mattel (Barbie, Hot Wheels, Matchbox).

The information in this book is given in good faith; however, no warranty is given, nor are results guaranteed. Your safety is your responsibility. Neither Spring House Press nor the authors assume any responsibility for any injuries or accidents.

To learn more about Spring House Press books, or to find a retailer near you, email info@springhousepress.com or visit us at www.springhousepress.com.

small
box crafts

Dioramas, Doll Rooms + Toy-Sized Spaces
for Imaginative Play

Designed by
Christen Byrd

Written by
Susan White Sullivan

SPRING HOUSE PRESS

contents

introduction

We've all heard the story about the child who opened a gift, pushed the contents aside, and proceeded to play with the empty box for hours. What is it about boxes that are so appealing? Perhaps they allow the imagination space to create a story all its own!

Although Christen is a designer of all things creative, her first box play space—the family room + kitchen—was created for her three kiddos, Lucy, Olive, and Max. It caught the eye of her craft book editor friend Susan, who said, "Wow, I think that could be a fun book!" And off they went, with Christen designing spaces and Susan writing instructions and drawing diagrams and patterns.

Creating the box spaces in this book is simple and affordable. The majority of the projects here were created with the storage boxes you can find in your local craft store. A few of the projects utilize a shipping box or other cardboard container. A glue gun is essential and was used for almost every bit of construction. Next, you can shop your craft stash or your local craft store for embellishments: fabric, paint, wooden dowel rods and shapes, decorative paper, felt, balsa wood, floral wire, beads, jewelry findings, ribbon, and on and on.

The sky's the limit when it comes to decorating your space. The instructions with each space are very detailed—follow them to the letter, or treat them as a jumping-off point and totally wing it! It's all up to you! Before you know it, you'll have completed one of the nine spaces featured in this book—Ballet Studio, Ice Cream Shoppe, Rocket Ship, Superhero Hideout, Farm, Fairy Garden, Bedroom, Auto Center, or the one that started it all: the Family Room + Kitchen. Oh, and one more plus. When the kids are finished playing they can load up all of the furniture and accessories into the box and close the lid!

Both Christen and Susan hope that you will involve the kids in the construction of these magical spaces. Let them help you with the parts they can handle. Yes, you'll be the glue gun wielder, but they can handle so many bits and if they're allowed to be involved, they will really own their play spaces. The goal is not perfection, but a place for little imaginations to dream big dreams! Happy creating!

tools & materials

GLUE GUN

Every piece of cardboard, paper, fabric, felt, and bead in this book was attached with a hot glue gun. These days, you can buy a glue gun for just a few bucks. Don't forget the glue sticks. If you haven't used a glue gun before, handling it safely is of the utmost importance! Follow the manufacturer's instructions to the letter.

OTHER TOOLS

We didn't really use too many other tools; a craft knife, scissors, paper punches, and paintbrushes are all you will need.

BOXES

No surprise here—you'll need a box! We recommend the decorative boxes from the craft store that have magnetic closures because they are convenient and look nice. However, you can use any kind of box or container—it doesn't have to be a square. Any shipping box or packaging that is large enough to hold your dream space will do. For example, the Rocket Ship (page 64) is made from a large old-fashioned oatmeal container!

Instructions for each play space give the exact dimensions of the box that was used in the photography, but there's a good chance you won't have that exact size. No worries! Make it up as you go along. It's all about having a good time.

OTHER SUPPLIES

There's a good chance you will have most of the supplies you need in your very own craft closet, but your local craft store will certainly be happy to be your creative partner-in-crime. Each space has a complete materials list, but here's an idea of the types of supplies used:

- Boxes
- Decorative paper: scrapbook, cardstock, gift wrap
- Acrylic paint
- Permanent pen/marker
- Packing tape
- Felt
- Tracing paper (to make patterns)
- Fabric and tulle
- Ribbon
- Washi tape
- Artificial flowers and greenery
- Sticks
- Twine
- Fiberfill stuffing
- Wooden dowel rods and shapes
- Balsa wood sheets
- Jewelry findings
- Beads
- Tea lights (battery operated)

ballet studio

En pointe... plié... pirouette! Let this charming studio fuel a young person's imagination as they imagine dancing on the big stage.

preparing the box

MATERIALS + SUPPLIES

- Decorative box with magnetic closure, 9½ x 7 x 4 in.
- Sheet silver metallic paper, 8 x 10 in. (back wall)
- Sheet floral scrapbook paper, 12 x 12 in. (side walls and banner triangles)
- Baker's twine (or any small string or yarn), 12 in.
- Sheet white-washed woodgrain scrapbook paper, 12 x 12 in. (floor)
- Wooden dowel, 8½ x 3/16 in. (barre)
- Piece of balsa wood, 3 x ¾ x ⅛ in. (bench top)
- (2) pieces of balsa wood, ⅜ x 1 x ⅛ in. (bench legs)
- Hot glue gun and glue sticks
- Scissors

INSTRUCTIONS

1 Open box and position with lid on table. Glue silver paper to cover the back wall. Glue floral paper to side walls, reserving excess paper for banner triangles. Glue woodgrain paper to floor.

2 For the bench, glue top piece to legs. Referring to photo for placement, glue legs to floor.

3 For barre, position dowel 2½ inches from floor and glue in place. If you have a pair of small fancy brackets, glue one on each end to look like a support bracket. Otherwise, just gluing the dowel to the wall works fine.

4 For the banner, cut seven triangles (⅝-inch at wide end and ¾-inch tall) from floral paper and glue to twine; refer to photo to glue the banner in place.

ballerina instructor

FINISHED SIZE

Approx. 4½-in. tall

MATERIALS + SUPPLIES

- Wooden clothespin doll, 4¼ in.
- White acrylic paint
- Metallic gold acrylic paint
- Paintbrush
- Black fine-tip permanent marker
- (3) pieces pale green net, 1¾ x 33 in. (tutu)
- Sewing needle and thread
- Bead, ¼-in. diameter (bun)

INSTRUCTIONS

PAINTING

1 Glue bead to back of head for bun. If you use enough glue, when you place it on the head and push in, the glue will squish out under the bead and look like the bun has a ring around it.

2 Paint hair and bun with gold metallic paint. Use permanent black marker for eyes.

3 Paint the white bodice, starting at the waist (2½ inches from the feet) and make it about ¾ inch tall to the top of the bodice. Allow paint to dry.

TUTU

1 Align the three layers of net into a stack.

2 Thread needle and make a running stitch through all three layers along one long edge.

3 Gather net by pulling the thread. Measure to instructor's waist. Tie off thread to secure net at desired length.

4 Glue the tutu to the waist at approximately 2½ inches above the feet.

ballerinas

FINISHED SIZE

Approx. 2¾-in. tall

MATERIALS + SUPPLIES

For each ballerina:

- Wooden peg doll, 1¾ x ⅝-in. diameter (upper body)
- Wooden candle cup, ¾ x ½-in. diameter (lower body)
- (3) pieces pale green or pink net, 1½ x 36 in. (tutu)
- Bead, ³⁄₁₆-in. diameter (bun, optional)
- White acrylic paint
- Metallic gold acrylic paint
- Paintbrush
- Black fine-tip permanent marker
- Sewing needle and thread
- Hot glue gun and glue sticks

INSTRUCTIONS

1 Follow the instructions for painting the instructor (page 12). Keep in mind buns are optional for the ballerinas.

2 Glue the candle cup to the bottom of the doll to create legs.

3 Follow the instructions for creating the instructor's tutu (page 12).

chandelier

FINISHED SIZE

Approx. 2-in. tall x 1¼-in. diameter

MATERIALS + SUPPLIES

- **(6) French hook earring wires**
- **Ball-end head pin, 2 in.**
- **Pink bead, ½-in. diameter**
- **(7) clear faceted beads, ⅜-in. diameter**
- **(4) cream beads, ³⁄₁₆-in. diameter**
- **(4) pink beads, ³⁄₁₆-in. diameter**
- **Wire cutter and pliers**
- **Hot glue gun and glue sticks**

NOTE

This project is so cute, but it is probably the most complex item in the book. It is helpful to use fresh glue sticks and a small glue gun with a small tip. Note the step images show slightly different beads than the finished project.

INSTRUCTIONS

1 Make the chandelier arms. Using the pliers, bend the four French earring wires so that the curve is a U shape instead of a more closed curve. Also, twist the eye loops so they are perpendicular to the curve. In the photo of this step, the top hook has been modified.

2 Add beads to each arm. Add a cream bead, a clear bead, and a small pink bead. Secure top bead with glue. Repeat to make four arms.

3 Place a faceted bead and then the ½-inch-diameter bead on the head pin.

4 Slide the four arm loops onto the head pin. Slide one faceted bead onto the head pin. Arrange the arms so they are evenly spaced around the large bead. Push the faceted bead against the arms to hold them in place; apply glue and hold until glue hardens. Slide the remaining faceted bead onto the head pin. Bend top of head pin into a loop. Attach a French earring wire for hanging.

5 Glue the last French earring wire flat against the ceiling of the studio, allowing enough space between the wire and the ceiling to hang the chandelier.

tote bag

FINISHED SIZE

1½-in. long x 1¾-in. tall

MATERIALS + SUPPLIES

- Fabric, 2 x 4 in.
- ½-in.-wide ribbon, 3 in.
- Hot glue gun and glue sticks
- Scissors

INSTRUCTIONS

1 Fold and finger-press all raw edges of fabric piece ¼ inch to wrong side.

2 Placing wrong sides together, fold fabric piece in half, matching short edges.

3 Leaving end open, glue front and back together along side edges.

4 For handle, glue ends of ribbon piece to inside of tote.

bedroom

A place of one's own... This cool bedroom has it all, including a teepee! Decorating this fun space could be the inspiration to an interior design career.

preparing the box

MATERIALS+ SUPPLIES

- Decorative box with magnetic closure, 16½ x 11½ x 5¼ in.
- Decorative or wrapping paper, 16½ x 11½ in. (back wall)
- Sheet scrapbook paper, 12 x 12 in. (side walls)
- Sheet scrapbook paper, 12 x 12 in. (area rug)
- Cardstock, 1¾ x 10 in. (light fixture)
- Washi tape, ¼ x 10 in. (light fixture)
- Mirror, 3-in. diameter
- Twine, 12 in. (banner)
- Multiple colors washi tape, ¼ x ½ in. (banner)
- Decorative paper, 4-in. square (pennant)
- Washi tape, ¼ x 2-in. (pennant)
- Scrapbook paper or magazine image with framed artwork (picture)
- Fabric flower, 1¼-in. diameter, purchased
- Hot glue gun and glue sticks
- Scissors

INSTRUCTIONS

1 Open box and position with lid on table. Cut papers for back and side walls to size and glue. Cut a 12 x 10-inch area rug and glue to inside of lid.

2 For light fixture, apply washi tape to one long edge of cardstock. Match short edges and overlap so that you have a 3-inch diameter circle and glue closed. Glue to ceiling.

3 Refer to photo for placement and glue mirror to wall.

4 For banner, cut ½-inch lengths of washi tape and fold over twine, spaced as desired. Refer to photo for placement and glue in place on back wall.

5 For pennants, cut two triangles from decorative paper 1½ inches wide at base and 2½ inches long. Add washi tape along base. Glue to wall.

6 The framed art was cut from scrapbook paper that had the frame printed on it. If you don't find something like this, you can cut out framed art from magazines or draw your own. Glue in place.

7 Glue flower to frame.

dresser

FINISHED SIZE

6-in. long x 2-in. wide x 3⅜-in. tall

MATERIALS + SUPPLIES

- Cardboard box, 6 x 3⅜ x 1⅞ in.
- (2) sheets balsa wood, ⅛ x 1½ x 6 in. (drawers)
- (2) arrow thumbtacks (handles)
- Washi tape, ⅝ x 6 in.
- Piece heavy cardstock, 6 x 6 in. (magazines)
- Washi tape, ¼ x 12 in. (magazines)
- Hot glue gun and glue sticks
- Scissors

INSTRUCTIONS

1 Glue balsa wood pieces to front of box (we used an iPhone box top).

2 Push thumbtacks into wood for handles.

3 Apply washi tape to top of box.

4 For magazines, cut cardstock into 2 x 1½-inch pieces. Fold in half to 1 x 1½ inches. Decorate with washi tape.

rug

FINISHED SIZE

4-in. diameter

MATERIALS + SUPPLIES

- White cardboard, 4-in. diameter
- (80) white pompoms, ⅜-in. diameter
- Hot glue gun and glue sticks
- Scissors

INSTRUCTIONS

Starting in the center and working outward, glue pompoms to cardboard.

bed, bedding + pillows

FINISHED SIZES

Bed, 7⅞-in. long x 5-in. wide x 4⅜-in. tall
Bedspread, 7¼-in. long x 9-in. wide
Pink pillow, 3½-in. long x 2½-in. wide
Grey pillow, 5½-in. long x 3-in. wide

MATERIALS + SUPPLIES

- Cardboard box, 4¾ x 7½ x 2¼ in. (bed)
- Fabric, ¼ yd. x 44 in. (cover box)
- (2) sheets balsa wood, ⅛ x 5 x 3 in. (foot and headboard)
- Fabric, 11 x 9 in. (bedspread)
- Pink fabric, 4½ x 6 in. (pillow)
- Grey fabric, 6½ x 7 in. (pillow)
- Fiberfill, 2 oz. (stuffing)
- Hot glue gun and glue sticks
- Scissors

INSTRUCTIONS

1 Cover box with fabric and glue to bottom of box.

2 Glue footboard to one end of bed flush with bottom of box. Glue headboard approximately 1½ inches from bottom of box.

3 For bedspread, place on bed to be sure the size is right in case your box is a slightly different size. Finger-press each edge 1 inch to the wrong side and glue in place.

4 For each pillow, with wrong sides facing, fold fabric in half, matching short edges. Glue fabrics together using ½-inch seam on both short ends, corners, and slightly into the long edges (leaving an opening to turn and stuff). Let glue cool and turn pillow right side out.

5 Stuff pillows with fiberfill and glue opening closed.

teepee

FINISHED SIZE

Approx. 6-in. tall x 17-in. diameter at base

MATERIALS + SUPPLIES

- (3) wooden dowel rods, 6 x ⅜ in. diameter (teepee legs)
- Fabric, 8 x 10 in.
- Washi tape, 24 x ¼ in.
- Twine, 3 yd.
- Hot glue gun and glue sticks
- Scissors

INSTRUCTIONS

1   Using pattern (page 21), cut teepee fabric piece.

2   Apply washi tape to staight edges of fabric piece.

3   To contruct the teepee frame, position legs at top end as shown and with feet about 4¾-inch distance between. Glue in place. Wrap twine around glued area.

Photo 1

4   Position the fabric piece around dowels, overlapping at the top front. Glue in place at top of legs and overlap of fabric.

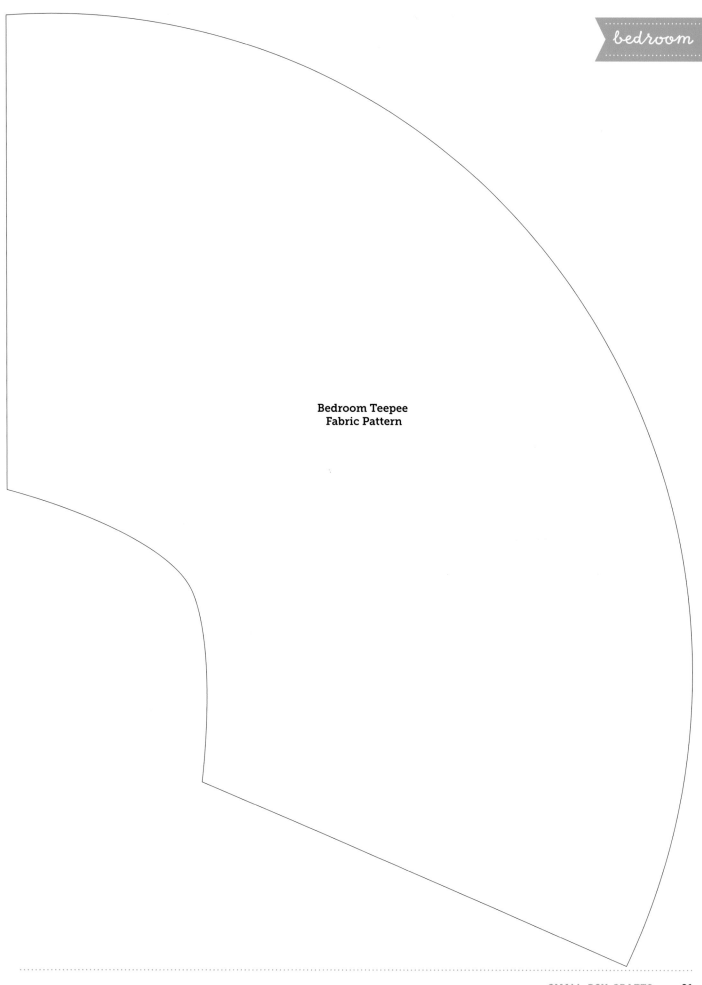

Bedroom Teepee
Fabric Pattern

storage containers

FINISHED SIZE

White, 2¼-in. tall x 1¾-in. diameter

Gray, 1½-in. tall x 1½-in. diameter

MATERIALS + SUPPLIES

- White fabric, 6½ x 5 in.
- Gray fabric, 6½ x 3½ in.
- Paper towel roll, 2½-in. length
- Paper towel roll, 1½-in. length
- Permanent black marker (optional)
- Hot glue gun and glue sticks
- Scissors

INSTRUCTIONS

1. Center the larger piece of paper towel roll on the white fabric so there is a 1-inch overhang at the top and bottom of the roll. Wrap fabric around roll, overlapping fabric; glue in place.

2. For bottom edge, turn fabric in on itself and glue in place (see photo). Turn excess fabric into container.

3. If desired, draw eyes on container.

4. Repeat process for gray container.

lamp

FINISHED SIZE

Approx. 7-in. tall

MATERIALS + SUPPLIES

- Wooden cone, 1¼-in. diameter at base x 2 in. tall
- Wooden dowel rod, 5 x ⅜-in. diameter
- Clear plastic medicine bottle, 2 x 1-in. diameter (lampshade)
- White cardstock, 4½ x 2¼ in. (lampshade)
- Scrapbook paper, 4½ x 2¼ in. (lampshade)
- Hot glue gun and glue sticks
- Scissors

INSTRUCTIONS

1   Bottle should be 1⅞ inches tall. Trim if needed.

2   Glue dowel rod into cone.

3   Center and glue other end of dowel rod onto the inside bottom of the bottle.

4   Match the long end of the cardstock to the open end of the bottle and glue the cardstock around the bottle, including the overlapping short ends.

5   Glue the scrapbook paper to cover the cardstock.

family room
+ kitchen

Put your feet up... Chill out in the family room while Mom's whipping up snacks in the kitchen. And guess what? The lights over the bar really work!

preparing the box

MATERIALS + SUPPLIES

- Decorative box with magnetic closure, 15½ x 14 x 4 in.
- Copy of kitchen artwork (pages 34 and 35)
- (2) sheets gold metallic scrapbook paper, 12 x 12 in. (wallpaper)
- (2) sheets woodgrain scrapbook paper, 12 x 12 in. (living room floor)
- Unfinished wooden box, 6¼ x 9 x 1½ in. (island)
- Hot glue gun and glue sticks
- Scissors

INSTRUCTIONS

1. Open box and position with lid on table.

2. Glue cabinet/counter artwork to back and side walls (see pages 34 and 35), referring to photo for placement.

3. Glue gold metallic paper for wallpaper to back and side walls. Glue window artwork in place.

4. Set island aside to put in place when assembling the room.

curtains

INSTRUCTIONS

1. On the outer edges of the dowel, wrap and glue each fabric panel over dowel, allowing a 1-inch overlap on wrong side.

2. Tie each panel with decorative cord and trim excess.

FINISHED SIZE

Each panel 5 in. long x 2 in. wide

MATERIALS + SUPPLIES

- (2) fabric pieces, 2 x 6 in.
- Wooden dowel, 5½ x ³⁄₁₆-in. diameter
- Decorative cord, 12 in.
- Hot glue gun and glue sticks
- Scissors

fridge

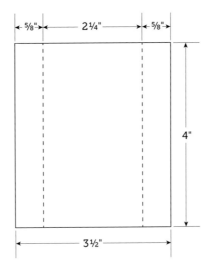

Fridge Support Diagram

FINISHED SIZE

Approx. 4½-in. wide x 10-in. tall

MATERIALS + SUPPLIES

- **Cardboard, 9⅞ x 4½ in. (fridge door)**
- **Cardboard, 3½ x 4 in. (back support)**
- **Sheet scrapbook paper, 12 x 12 in. (fridge front)**
- **Metal clip from ball point pen (handle)**
- **Hot glue gun and glue sticks**
- **Craft knife**

INSTRUCTIONS

1 From cardboard, cut out the fridge door to the size indicated in the materials list and the back support as shown in the diagram (at left). Referring to photo, round corners of door. Use cardboard door as pattern and cut the door front from scrapbook paper so it is slightly larger than the door.

2 For the back support, refer to the diagram and use the craft knife to cut through top layer only of cardboard along the dashed lines. Fold along cut lines and glue the support to the back of the door.

3 Glue scrapbook paper door front to cardboard door.

4 Glue metal clip to door.

5 Glue completed fridge to back wall of kitchen.

tea light pendants

FINISHED SIZE (NOT INCLUDING WIRE)

Each approx. 1½ in. tall x 1½-in. diameter

MATERIALS + SUPPLIES

- Ribbon, 5½ x 1½ in.
- (2) battery-operated tea lights, 1¼-in. diameter
- Floral wire, 26 gauge x 10 in.
- Hot glue gun and glue sticks
- Scissors

INSTRUCTIONS

1. Wrap ribbon around edge of tea light, with one long edge aligned with switch end. Glue in place.

2. Cut 4-inch-long piece of wire.

3. Curl one end of wire into flat piece and glue to tea light on switch end.

4. Curl other end of wire into flat piece and glue to ceiling of kitchen where desired.

5. Repeat steps to create second pendant.

kitchen shelves

FINISHED SIZE

Each approx. 4½ in. long x ¾ in. wide

MATERIALS + SUPPLIES

- (2) pieces balsa wood, 4½ x ¾ x ⅛ in. (shelves)
- Hot glue gun and glue sticks
- Decorative miniature plates and wooden bowls

INSTRUCTIONS

1   Glue shelves to wall.

2   Arrange dishes and glue in place.

coffee table + vase

FINISHED SIZE

Table, 1¾-in. tall x 4-in. diameter
Vase, 3½-in. tall with flower

MATERIALS + SUPPLIES

- Wooden spool, 1¾ x 4-in. diameter
- Washi tape, 1 yd. x ½-in.-wide
- Wooden cone, 1⅛-in. diameter base x 2 in. (vase)
- Small artificial flower

INSTRUCTIONS

1   Wrap washi tape around recessed center area of spool.

2   Insert flower in vase.

sofa

FINISHED SIZE

10¼-in. long x 3½-in. wide x 5½-in. tall

MATERIALS + SUPPLIES

- Cardboard, 16 x 20 in.
- Fabric, ¼ yd. x 44 to 45 in. wide
- Quilt batting, 1¾ x 10¼ in. (back cushioning)
- Quilt batting, 3¼ x 10⅛ in. (seat cushioning)
- Craft knife
- Hot glue gun and glue sticks
- Scissors

INSTRUCTIONS

1 Use solid lines on diagrams 1 and 2 (at left) to cut out cardboard pieces (dashed lines are fold lines after cutting out pieces).

2 For back and arm fabric, cut a 16 x 14-inch piece of fabric.

3 For seat fabric, cut a 12 x 14-inch piece of fabric.

4 Referring to dashed lines on diagrams 1 and 2, fold cardboard pieces as shown and cut through *outer layer only* of one side of the cardboard to easily fold and form arms/sides and seat.

5 Trim and glue cushion material to seat and shaded area on sofa back if desired.

6 Center and glue fabrics onto *folded* cardboard pieces, clipping where needed and wrapping excess to the back and underside.

7 Glue the seat/front piece to the back/sides.

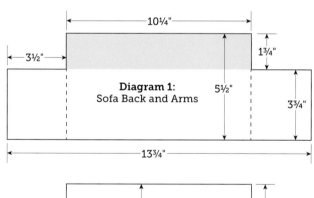

Diagram 1:
Sofa Back and Arms

10¼" · 3½" · 1¾" · 5½" · 3¾" · 13¾"

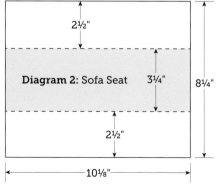

Diagram 2: Sofa Seat

2½" · 3¼" · 8¼" · 2½" · 10⅛"

chair

FINISHED SIZE

3¾-in. long x 3½-in. wide x 4½-in. tall

MATERIALS + SUPPLIES

- Cardboard, 11 x 13 in.
- Craft knife
- Fabric, ¼ yd. x 44 in.
- Hot glue gun and glue sticks

INSTRUCTIONS

1   Use solid lines on diagrams 1 and 2 (below) to cut out cardboard pieces (dashed lines are fold lines after cutting out pieces).

2   Cut a fabric piece 3 inches larger on both sides than each cardboard piece.

3   Referring to dashed lines on diagrams 1 and 2, fold cardboard pieces as shown and cut through *outer layer only* of one side of the cardboard to easily fold and form arms/sides and seat.

4   Center and glue fabrics onto *folded* cardboard pieces, clipping where needed and wrapping excess to the back and underside.

5   Glue the seat/front piece to the back/ sides.

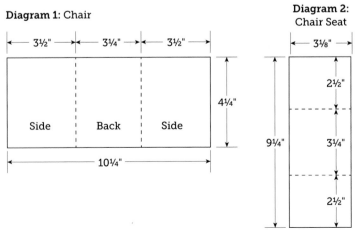

Diagram 1: Chair

← 3½" → ← 3¼" → ← 3½" →

| Side | Back | Side |

4¼"

← 10¼" →

Diagram 2: Chair Seat

← 3⅛" →

2½"

9¼"   3¼"

2½"

pillows

FINISHED SIZE

Polka dot, 2½-in. square
Gold print, 2½ x 3 in.

MATERIALS + SUPPLIES

- (2) pieces of polka dot fabric, 3 in. square
- (2) pieces of gold print fabric, 3 x 3½ in.
- Handful of fiberfill stuffing
- Hot glue gun and glue sticks
- Scissors

NOTE

You can make your pillows any size you like; just cut ½-inch larger than the finished size you want to accommodate seam allowances.

INSTRUCTIONS

1 To make the pillows as shown, cut two pieces of fabric to 3 x 3 inches, and two pieces from the second pattern of fabric to 3 x 3½ inches (see note).

2 Place wrong sides together and apply glue along three edges between the layers. Allow to cool.

3 Turn right side out and stuff with fiberfill to desired fullness.

4 Turn raw edges of pillow opening to the inside and apply glue to close.

pouf ottoman

FINISHED SIZE

2-in. tall x 4-in. diameter

MATERIALS + SUPPLIES

- Fabric, 6½ x 14 in.
- Fabric, 3½-in. diameter circle
- Cardboard, 2-in. diameter circle
- Fiberfill stuffing
- Hot glue gun and glue sticks
- Scissors

INSTRUCTIONS

1 With wrong sides together, fold larger fabric piece in half, matching short edges. Glue together along short edges.

2 Turn fabric tube right side out.

3 Determine how much stuffing you want in the ottoman to form it into the ottoman shape.

4 Place stuffing into tube and begin folding and gluing bottom edge of fabric toward the center of the ottoman. Repeat for top of ottoman, pleating and gluing as you go.

5 For top of ottoman, center cardboard circle on wrong side of fabric circle and glue excess to the back. Glue to center of ottoman top.

side table with attached lamp

FINISHED SIZE

5-in. tall x 2-in. diameter

MATERIALS + SUPPLIES

- Wooden cone, 2-in. tall x 1⅛-in. diameter at base (table base)
- Wooden circle, ¼ x 2-in. diameter (tabletop)
- Wooden bead, ⅞-in. diameter with ³⁄₁₆-in. diameter hole (lamp base)
- Plastic medicine cup as found with most children's cough syrup, 1½-in. tall x 1¼-in. diameter (lamp shade)
- Fabric, 5 x 2 in. (lamp shade cover)
- Wooden dowel, 1¾ in. x ³⁄₁₆-in. diameter (lamp stem)
- Gold acrylic paint
- Paintbrush
- Hot glue gun and glue sticks

INSTRUCTIONS

1 For table, glue narrow end of cone to center of circle.

2 For lamp base, paint bottom half of wooden bead with gold paint. Set bead aside.

3 The closed end of the cup will be the top of the lampshade. Wrap fabric piece around cup and determine how much to fold to the wrong side at the top and how much to fold to the inside of the cup at the bottom. Turn raw edge that runs the height of the cup to the wrong side. Glue all edges in place.

4 Glue one end of the dowel into the opening of the bead. Glue the other end of the dowel in center of the lampshade.

5 Glue lamp base to table.

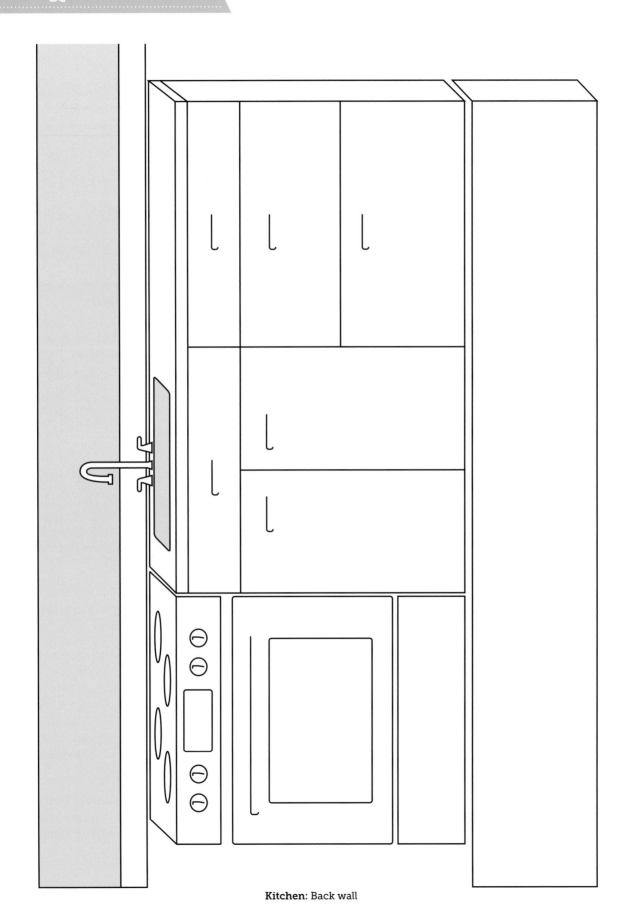

Kitchen: Back wall

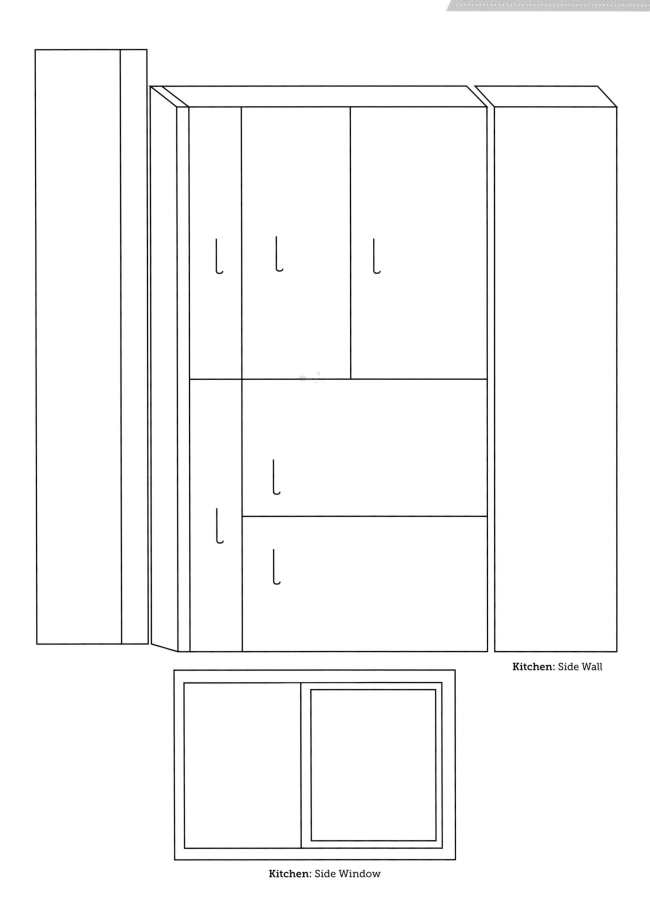

Kitchen: Side Wall

Kitchen: Side Window

ice cream shoppe

A double scoop of fun... **Who doesn't love ice cream? Make this fun shop to let the kiddos get their first taste of entrepreneurship!**

preparing the box

INSTRUCTIONS

1 Open box and position with lid on table. Glue printed paper to cover back wall. Glue white paper to side walls. Cut a 7½-inch square from the mint green paper and glue to inside of lid.

2 For each ice cream cone, cut a 3-inch square piece of kraft paper and roll into a cone. Trim so it's approximately 1½ inches tall, making sure the opening is large enough for the scoop.

3 For each ice cream scoop, paint wooden bead the desired color and glue into ice cream cone. Referring to photo for placement, glue cones to wall.

MATERIALS + SUPPLIES

- **Decorative box with magnetic closure, 8 x 8 x 5½ in.**
- **Sheet frozen treats printed scrapbook paper, 8 x 10 in. (back wall)**
- **Sheet white scrapbook paper, 8 x 10 in. (side walls)**
- **Sheet mint green scrapbook paper, 8 x 10 in. (floor)**
- **Sheet kraft paper, 8 x 10 in. (cones)**
- **(3) wooden beads, ½-in. diameter (ice cream scoops)**
- **Acrylic paint, assorted colors**
- **Paintbrush**
- **Hot glue gun and glue sticks**
- **Scissors**

ice cream counter

INSTRUCTIONS

1 For counter front, glue balsa wood to the front of the cardboard box. Be sure to position the open side of the box up.

2 For each ice cream carton, overlap short edges and glue in place (check to be sure they will fit inside the counter box before gluing).

3 For each ice cream cone, cut a 3-inch-square piece of kraft paper and roll into a cone. Trim so it's approximately 1½ inches tall, making sure the opening is large enough for the ice cream scoop bead. Glue cone overlapping edges together.

4 For each ice cream scoop, paint the wooden bead the desired color and glue into ice cream cone. Glue cones to counter.

FINISHED SIZE

Approx. 4⅔-in. long x 2½-in. wide x 3-in. tall

MATERIALS + SUPPLIES

- **Balsa wood, 4¾ x 3 x ⅛ in. (counter front)**
- **Cardboard box, 2 x 4 x 2¾ in. (open on one long side)**
- **(2) pieces white card stock, 2 x 5 in. (ice cream cartons)**
- **Sheet kraft paper, 8 x 10 in. (cones)**
- **(5) wooden beads, ½-in. diameter (ice cream scoops)**
- **Acrylic paint, assorted colors**
- **Paintbrush**
- **Hot glue gun and glue sticks**
- **Scissors**

ice cream server

FINISHED SIZE

Approx. 4½ in. tall

MATERIALS + SUPPLIES

- Wooden clothespin doll pin, 4¼ in.
- Metallic gold acrylic paint
- Paintbrush
- Bead, ¼-in. diameter (bun)
- Fabric, 3 in. square (apron)
- Washi tape, ¼ in. (straps)
- Hot glue gun and glue sticks
- Scissors

INSTRUCTIONS

1 Glue bead to head for bun and paint hair.

2 For apron skirt, cut a 1 x 2-inch piece of fabric. Fold in half, matching short ends. For apron bib, cut a 1 x ½-inch piece of fabric. Refer to photos for placement and use washi tape to attach fabric pieces to clothespin.

payment stand

FINISHED SIZE

Approx. 2-in. long x 1¾-in. wide x 4¾-in. tall (with register)

MATERIALS + SUPPLIES

- Balsa wood, 2 ¼ x 1 ¾ x ⅛ in.
- Cardboard, 4 x 8 in. (stand and register box)
- Piece of frozen treats scrapbook paper, 5 ½ x 2 ½ in. (to cover stand)
- Sheet of white cardstock, 8 x 10 in. (register support)
- Hot glue gun and glue sticks
- Scissors

INSTRUCTIONS

1. For payment table, cut a 5½ x 2½-inch piece of cardboard. Referring to diagram (below), score cardboard along dashed lines through top layer only and fold into a U shape. Cover stand with frozen treats paper. Glue balsa wood top to table.

2. For register stand, use cardboard to make a box 1 x 1 x ½ inches.

3. For register screen, cut a 1" x 1¼" piece from cardstock; round corners.

4. For register support, cut a cardstock strip ½ x 5 inches. Fold in half and then into a triangle (see photo at left) and glue to secure. Glue on screen and then glue to register stand.

Payment Table Diagram

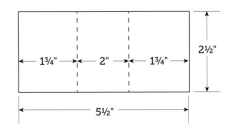

farm

Down on the farm... Growing veggies, tending cows, and plowing fields are not everyday activities for most kids. Let them have fun exploring farm life!

preparing the box

INSTRUCTIONS

1 Open box and position with lid on table. Glue the cloud scrapbook paper to cover the back wall.

2 For raised ground inside the box, cut a 7¼ x 6½-inch piece of cardboard. Fold across the width at 1½ and 5 inches.

3 Cut a piece of 7¼ x 6¾-inch green paper and glue to the raised ground piece. Slide ground into box and glue in place.

4 Glue fence to box in front of raised ground.

5 Cut and glue a piece of green paper to the lid. This serves as the barnyard.

MATERIALS + SUPPLIES

- Decorative box with magnetic closure, 7½ x 7½ x 4¼ in.
- Sheet of cloud scrapbook paper, 8 x 10 in.
- (2) sheets of green construction paper, 8 x 10 in.
- Cardboard, 8 x 10 in. (raised ground)
- Miniature fencing, approx. 2¼ x 7½ in.
- Variety of small plastic farm animals
- Hot glue gun and glue sticks
- Scissors

silo

FINISHED SIZE

Approx. 6-in. tall x ¾-in. diameter

MATERIALS + SUPPLIES

- Paper towel roll, 1¾-in. diameter, cut to 5¾-in. long
- Sheet of decorative paper to cover roll, 8 x 10 in.
- Hot glue gun and glue sticks
- Scissors

NOTE

The silo pictured was made from a 1¾-inch diameter plastic packaging container with a lid. You may have something around the house like this you can use.

INSTRUCTIONS

1 Cut paper to 5¾ x 6 inches.

2 Glue paper around roll.

barn

MATERIALS + SUPPLIES

- 1-pint milk carton
- Red acrylic paint
- White acrylic paint
- Paintbrush
- Sheet of white paper, 8 x 10 in. (barn door detail)
- Hot glue gun and glue sticks
- Scissors

INSTRUCTIONS

1 Paint barn roof white.

2 Paint barn sides red.

3 Referring to the barn door pattern (below), cut door detail from white paper and glue to a barn side.

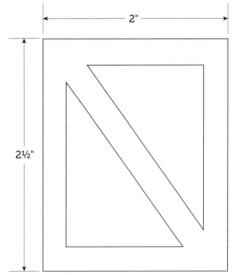

Barn Door Pattern

2"

2½"

garden

FINISHED SIZE

Approx. 4-in. long x 3-in. wide

MATERIALS + SUPPLIES

- Sheet of brown felt, 8 x 10 in.
- Sheet of green felt, 8 x 10 in.
- (5) oval orange beads, ⅜-in. long (carrots)
- Green floral wire, 26 gauge x 36 in.
- (3) wooden beads, ½-in. diameter (cabbages)
- Green acrylic paint
- Paintbrush
- Hot glue gun and glue sticks
- Scissors

INSTRUCTIONS

ROWS

1 Cut a 4 x 3 inch piece of brown felt for the base; cut a 5 x 4-inch piece of brown felt for garden rows.

2 On the 5 x 4-inch piece, mark the felt using the garden row diagram (at left). The dashed lines on the diagram indicate where the hot glue will be placed. Run a bead of hot glue down one marked line. Carefully fold along the bead of glue, encasing it in the fold. Repeat for each line. When you've glued each line and folded it on itself, you will have five rows with four glued lines.

3 Glue the row piece to the base. Trim any excess from the row piece if needed.

(continued on next page)

Garden Rows Diagram

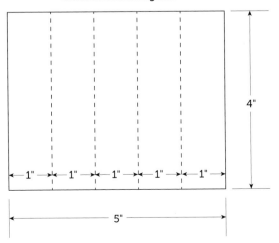

garden *(continued)*

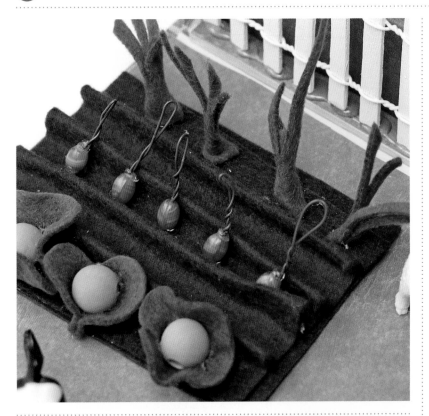

INSTRUCTIONS *(continued)*

CORN STALKS

1. Cut four ½ x 2-inch pieces from green felt.

2. Cut down the height of each piece several times. Trim the stalks to different lengths.

3. Roll each corn stalk lengthwise and glue the base of each stalk to the back row of the garden.

CARROTS

1. Cut five 1½-inch lengths of the green wire.

2. For each length, fold cut ends together and twist.

3. Glue cut ends into orange beads and glue beads to middle row of garden.

CABBAGES

1. Paint the three wooden beads green.

2. Cut three 1½-inch diameter circles from the green felt.

3. Glue each bead to the center of a felt circle, adding enough glue so you can pull the felt up the sides of the bead.

4. Glue the cabbage heads to the remaining outer row of garden.

tractor, pots + feeder

FINISHED SIZE

Approx. 4-in. long x 3-in. wide

MATERIALS + SUPPLIES

- Wooden chipboard tractor, approx. 4¼-in. wide x 3¼-in. high, purchased
- Cardboard scrap (tractor brace)
- Cardboard, 4-in. square (feeder)
- (2) wooden flower pots, ⅝-in. wide at top x ⅝-in. tall
- Scraps of brown and green felt
- Hot glue gun and glue sticks
- Scissors

INSTRUCTIONS

1 Make tractor brace by cutting a small triangle from cardboard. Glue to back (see photo at right).

2 Make pots by gluing green stands of felt in one pot and brown felt in the other.

3 Make feeder from cardboard by cutting a base 1⅛ x 1¼ inches. Cut four ½-inch-tall side pieces to fit base and glue in place.

superhero hideout

Super team, assemble! When the superheroes get together, they need a secret place to meet. This two-story hideout is perfect for planning to save the world!

preparing the box

Psst! The tube is a super-secret slide down to the first floor. Go ahead, try it out!

NOTE

There's a pretty good chance the box in your closet is not exactly the same size as the one we used for this project. Simply use the materials you have on hand and get inspired by our photos, instructions, and diagrams.

FINISHED SIZE

Approx. 14½-in. long x 11½-in. wide x 20-in. tall

MATERIALS + SUPPLIES

- Cardboard shipping box, 14½ x 8 x 7¼ in.
- Cardboard box with attached lid, 7½ x 4¾ x 2 in. (upper deck lounge)
- (2) sheets of scrapbook paper, 12 x 12 in. (floor)
- (2) sheets of scrapbook paper, 12 x 12 in. (back wall)
- (3) sheets of patterned paper, 8 x 10 in. (other areas)
- Sturdy cardboard tube, 16-in. long x 2¼-in. outside diameter with 2-in. diameter opening (transporter)
- (2) pieces of cardboard, 14 x 6 in. (tents)
- Scrapbook paper with graphics for BANG, BOING, and BOOM or draw your own
- Silver metallic cardboard letters P, O, and W, 2-in. tall
- Cardboard box, 5½ x 4 x ¾ in. (big screen TV/computer)
- Black and white print washi tape, ¾-in. wide
- Piece of red cardstock, 4-in. square (flag)
- Wooden dowel, 8-in. x ⅜-in. diameter (flag pole)
- Craft knife
- Packing tape
- Hot glue gun and glue sticks
- Scissors

preparing the box *(continued)*

INSTRUCTIONS

1 Cut and remove one long side flap of the shipping box. Lay box down with the long side that still has a flap against the table. Refer to the overhead view diagram (below) for the position of the transporter tube opening in the upper deck. Cut a 2¼-inch diameter circle as indicated for transporter tube.

2 Cover the floor and back wall of the lower floor with the appropriate scrapbook papers.

3 For the upper deck lounge, open the smaller box's lid and position it on the far left edge of the upper deck. Fold front tab to the inside of the box and glue the box in place. Use decorative papers to cover the floor and back wall.

4 Cut out (or draw, color, and cut out your own) BANG, BOING, and BOOM graphics and glue to the back walls of the lower level and upper deck lounge.

5 For each tent, fold a cardboard piece into a tent measuring 3 ¾ inches on each side and 5 inches across the bottom. You will have a double layer on one 3¾-inch side. Glue in place.

6 For the tent on top of the transporter tube, draw a 2¼-inch diameter circle centered on the 5-inch bottom. Cut out. Insert tube in opening and use packing tape to secure the tent to the tube.

7 Cover the transporter tent with paper and glue the "POW" letters on one side of tent.

Overhead View

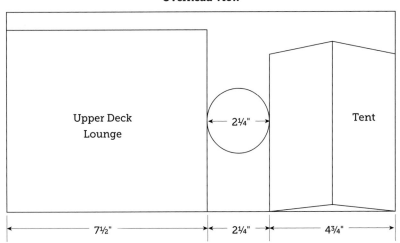

8   Glue the remaining tent to the upper deck to the right of the transporter opening. Cut a piece of paper to go inside the tent. Glue in place.

9   For the flag, cut a triangle from red paper approximately 2½ inches at the base and 4 inches long. Glue to one end of the flag pole. Make a hole in the tent roof and slide the flag pole in.

10 For the big screen TV/computer, cut a piece of decorative paper the size of the TV box. Use washi tape to secure paper to box, cover the sides, and create a frame. Glue box to wall.

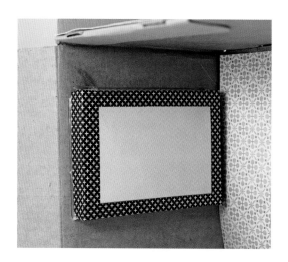

couch

FINISHED SIZE

Approx. 6¼-in. long x 2½-in. wide x 2½-in. tall

MATERIALS + SUPPLIES

- Cardboard, 12 x 6 in. (couch frame)
- Fabric, ¼ yd. x 44 in.
- (4) wooden flower pots, ⅝-in. wide at top x ⅝-in. tall (couch legs)
- Hot glue gun and glue sticks
- Scissors

INSTRUCTIONS

1 Use the pattern of the sofa back and arms (page 51) to cut out the pattern from cardboard along the solid lines. The dashed lines on the pattern indicate fold lines. Fold back and arms along dashed lines and glue the arms to back. Tip: It is really helpful to cut with the craft knife through the top layer only of the cardboard along the dashed lines: it makes folding the cardboard so much easier.

2 Cut two fabric pieces: 15 x 4 inches for the seat and arms and 10 x 6 inches for the back and front.

3 Center the seat and arm fabric on top of the couch. Smooth the fabric and secure it by gluing fabric along back edge of the seat and where the seat meets the arms.

4 On each side, clip from the front edge of the fabric to the front edge of the seat where the seat meets the arms. Wrap the fabric around the arm from the inside to the outside and glue in place.

5 Wrap both layers of arm fabric over the top of the arm and around to the bottom; glue in place. Repeat for remaining arm. Fold fabric along the front edge of seat to the bottom and glue in place.

6 For the couch seat and back, take the remaining fabric piece and center on couch, positioning it so that the edges overlap on the bottom of the couch. Start gluing on the front where the seat and back meet. Continue to glue to secure the fabric to the couch as needed. Glue legs to couch.

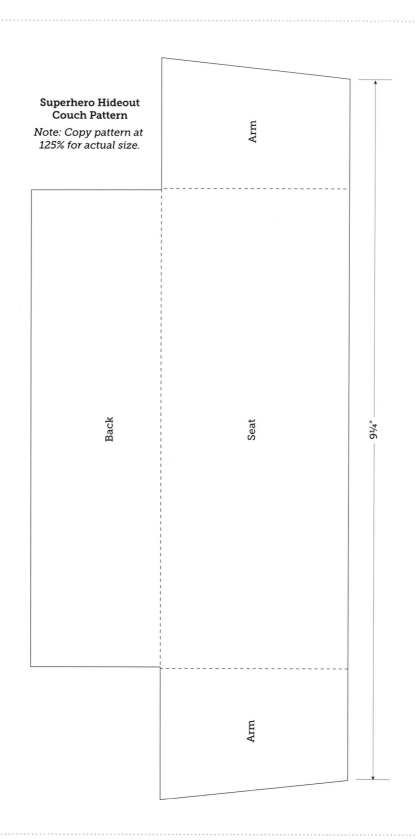

**Superhero Hideout
Couch Pattern**

*Note: Copy pattern at
125% for actual size.*

Arm

Back

Seat

9¼"

Arm

That new car feeling... Tune-ups and car washes will be a snap with this cool auto center. Finally, the perfect home and play space for all of those toy cars!

preparing the box

NOTE

There's a pretty good chance the box in your closet is not exactly the same size as the one we used for this project. Simply use the materials you have on hand and get inspired by our photos, instructions, and diagrams.

FINISHED SIZE

Approx. 28-in. long x 21-in. wide x 5½-in. tall

MATERIALS + SUPPLIES

- Cardboard shipping box, 13½ x 11 x 4¾ in.
- Sheet patterned scrapbook paper, 12 x 12 in. (back wall)
- (3) wooden fan handles, 8-in. long (reinforcing floor)
- Craft knife
- Packing tape
- Hot glue gun and glue sticks
- Scissors
- Black and white striped washi tape
- Yellow washi tape

INSTRUCTIONS

1 Referring to diagrams 1, 2, and 3, open the box and remove flaps. On one side, cut box where ends and sides meet to release the side/top so it can lay flat on the table. Use packing tape to re-attach the opposite top to the ends.

2 Cover back wall with scrapbook paper.

3 Cut a 5 x 13¼-inch piece of black scrapbook paper (piecing as needed) and glue to the top of the box. Use black and white striped washi tape to create lanes and cover edges. Use the yellow washi tape to create center lines.

4 Referring to photo (at left), glue three fan handles on the bottom of the box to support the part that rests on the table.

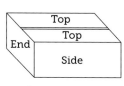

Diagram 1

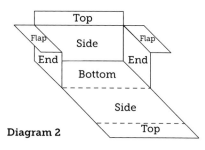

Diagram 2

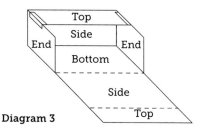

Diagram 3

car wash

MATERIALS + SUPPLIES

- Cardboard, 5 x 7½ in.

- Fabric, 4-in. square (car wash scrubbers)

- White cardstock, 1 x 4 in. (car wash sign)

- Black permanent marker

- Sheet patterned scrapbook paper (front left wall)

- Hot glue gun and glue sticks

- Scissors

- Sheet black scrapbook paper, 12 x 12 in. (top)

INSTRUCTIONS

1 Referring to diagram 4, cut out door from the cardboard piece and bend along dashed lines.

2 For scrubbers, cut fabic in ¼-inch strips, stopping ½-inch from the top. Center and glue inside, above opening.

3 With top and bottom pieces of door folded toward scrubbers, glue folded pieces to top and bottom of box.

4 Using black marker, write CAR WASH on the white cardstock and glue over door opening.

5 Cover front left wall with patterned scrapbook paper.

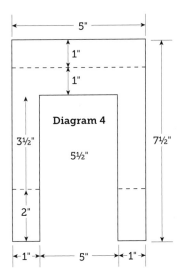

Diagram 4

5"

1"

1"

3½"

5½"

7½"

2"

1"   5"   1"

car wash tunnel + parking

MATERIALS + SUPPLIES

- Sheet black and white striped scrapbook paper, 12 x 12 in.
- (2) sheets black scrapbook paper, 12 x 12 in.
- Sheet green scrapbook paper, 12 x 12 in.
- Yellow washi tape, ¼-in. wide
- Cardboard roll from wrapping paper, 2½-in. diameter
- Green and white striped washi tape, ¾-in. wide
- Black and white polka dotted washi tape, ¼-in. wide

INSTRUCTIONS

1 Referring to photo (at left) for placement, cut and glue the following from scrapbook paper:

- Green, 4 x 10 in. (grass)
- Black, 7½ x 10½ in. (parking spaces)
- (2) pieces of black and white stripe, 2 x 12 in. (sidewalk)
- (2) pieces of black, 2 x 12 in. (road)

2 Use yellow washi tape to add driving lane center stripe and parking lines.

3 Cut tube lengthwise to open. Position over driving lane to determine how much you need to remove. Cut away excess. Use green and white washi tape to decorate tunnel. Glue tunnel in place.

4 Use black and white polka dotted washi tape to create arrows coming out of car wash door.

ramp

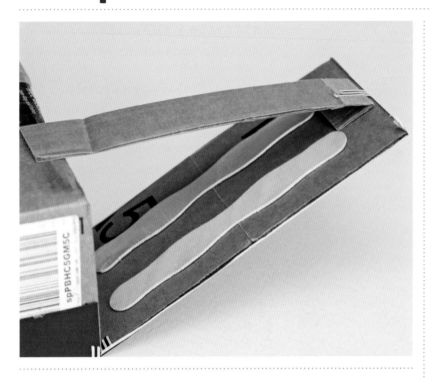

MATERIALS + SUPPLIES

- Cardboard, 5 x 10 in. (ramp)
- Cardboard, 2 x 12 in. (reinforcement)
- Sheet black scrapbook paper, 12 x 12 in.
- Black and white striped washi tape, ¾-in. wide
- Yellow washi tape, ¼-in. wide
- (2) wooden fan handles, 8-in. long (reinforcing ramp)
- Hot glue gun and glue sticks
- Scissors

INSTRUCTIONS

1 Cover ramp with black scrapbook paper. Use black and white striped washi tape to create lanes and cover edges. Use the yellow washi tape to create center lines.

2 Glue ramp to right side of box and cover glue with washi tape.

3 Glue two fan handles to back of ramp for reinforcement. Fold one end of cardboard reinforcement piece 1 inch from end. Glue the folded inch to the bottom of the ramp and the other end to the bottom of box.

clean out + vacuum area

NOTE

This area is created by using the side of the box as the wall of the clean out/vacuum area.

MATERIALS + SUPPLIES

- (2) pieces of cardboard, 5 x 10½ in. (floor and roof)
- Sheet patterned scrapbook paper, 12 x 12 in. (clean out/vacuum area)
- Sheet black and white striped scrapbook paper, 12 x 12 in. (cover floor and roof)
- (3) wooden dowels, 4¾ x ⅜-in. diameter
- Cardboard, 5¾ x ¾ in. (upper parking area wall)
- Black and white patterned washi tape, ¾-in. wide
- (2) pieces of cardboard, 1 x 3 in. (trashcans)
- Yellow washi tape, ¼-in. wide
- (2) wooden fan handles, 8-in. long (reinforcment)
- Hot glue gun and glue sticks
- Scissors

INSTRUCTIONS

1 Cover the wall with patterned scrapbook paper and one side of each of the floor and roof with black and white scrapbook paper.

2 Referring to photo for placement, glue the three dowels to the floor approximately 1 inch from one long edge and 1½ inches in from short ends. Repeat to glue other end to roof so the dowels are glued in same position on roof. Glue opposite long edges of floor and roof to corresponding edges of the box wall.

3 Glue the cardboard wall for the top parking area to the edge at front side of box. Cover with patterned washi tape.

4 Cover edges of floor, wall, and roof with patterned washi tape.

5 For trash cans, fold each cardboard piece and glue each into a triangle. Glue open end to floor.

6 Use yellow washi tape to create parking lines on roof.

7 On the bottom, glue two fan handles across the box and clean out/vacuum area for reinforcement.

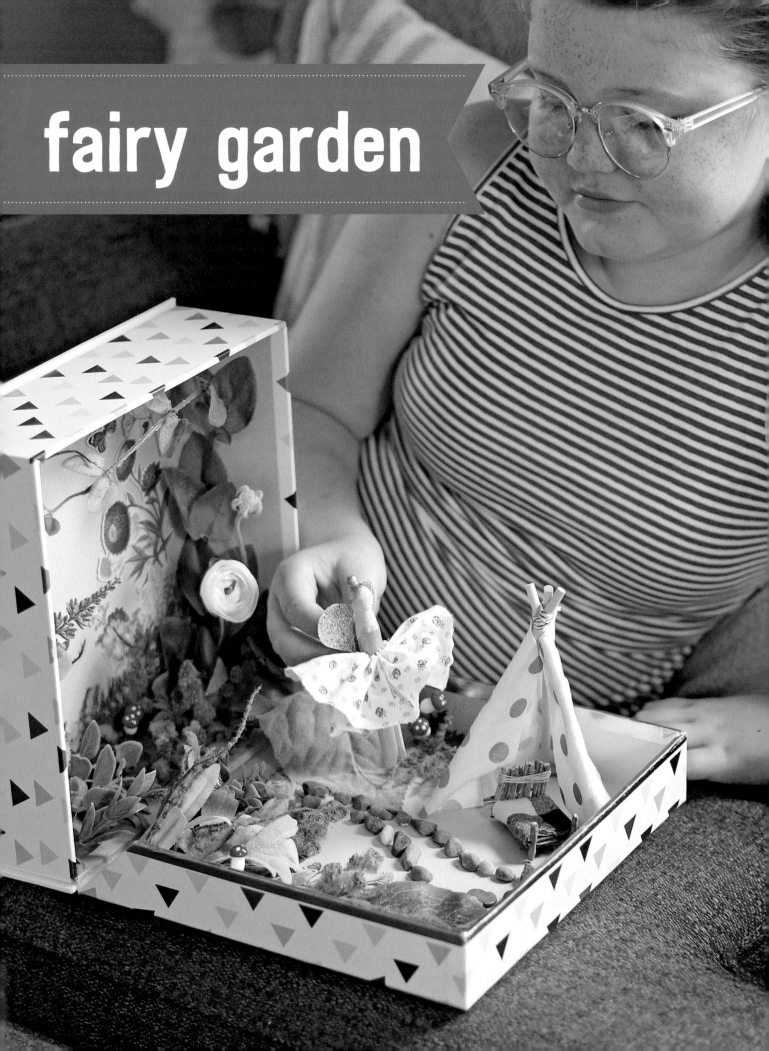

fairy garden

Into the woods... Create a magical space for fairies, gnomes, and woodland creatures. Follow the path to a woodland paradise!

preparing the box

MATERIALS + SUPPLIES

- Decorative box with attached lid, 10 x 10 x 4 in.
- Decorative paper with realistic flowers, butterflies, and birds that can be cut out and applied to back wall
- A variety of artificial flowers, ferns, and leaves
- (12) mini mushroom stems, ⅝-in. tall on a 3-in. floral wire stem
- (30) small rocks, ½ to ¾-in. long (path)
- Hot glue gun and glue sticks
- Scissors

INSTRUCTIONS

1 Open box and position with lid on table. Cut out and glue paper flowers, butterflies, and birds to back wall.

2 Decide path direction and glue rocks in place on lid.

3 Layer and glue ferns and leaves to lid and inside box. Glue flowers in place.

4 Glue mushroom stems in a varity of spots on lid and inside box.

fairy

FINISHED SIZE

Approx. 4½-in. tall

MATERIALS + SUPPLIES

- Wooden clothespin doll pin, 4¼-in. tall
- Wooden bead, ¼-in. diameter (bun)
- Metallic gold acrylic paint
- Paintbrush
- Fabric, 26 x 2 in. (skirt)
- Glittered heavy paper, 3-in. square (wings)
- Sewing needle and thread
- Hot glue gun and glue sticks
- Scissors

INSTRUCTIONS

1 Glue bead to back of head for bun. If you use enough glue, when you place the bead on the head and push in, the glue will squish out under the bead and look like the bun has a ring around it.

2 Referring to photo, paint hair, bun, and bodice. The bodice should start about 2 ½ inches from the feet.

3 For skirt, thread needle with thread and make a running stitch through one long edge of fabric.

4 Gather fabric by pulling the thread. Measure to fit the waist, overlapping the short ends. Tie off thread to secure skirt at desired length.

5 Glue the skirt to the waist at appoximately 2½ inches above the feet.

6 Cut the fairy wing pattern from the glittered paper. With unglittered side coming together, fold along center of pattern and glue in place on back of the fairy.

Fairy Wing Pattern

teepee

FINISHED SIZE

Approx. 6-in. tall x 14-in. diameter at base

MATERIALS + SUPPLIES

- (3) wooden dowel rods, 6 x ⅜-in. diameter (teepee legs)
- Fabric, 8 x 10 in.
- Twine, 3 yd.
- Hot glue gun and glue sticks
- Scissors

INSTRUCTIONS

1 Using pattern (page 21), cut teepee fabric piece.

2 To contruct the teepee frame, position legs crossed at top end. At opposite end, the legs should be approximately 4 inches apart. Glue in place. Wrap twine around glued area.

3 Position fabric piece around dowels and glue in place at top of legs, with fabric wrapped to the inside.

fairy bed

FINISHED SIZE

Approx. 2-in. long x 1½-in. wide
x 1½-in. tall

MATERIALS + SUPPLIES

- Stick(s), ¼ to ⅜-in. diameter, approx.
  24 in. total length
- Fabric, 1¾ x 3½ in. (bedding)
- Twine, 10 in.
- Hot glue gun and glue sticks
- Scissors

INSTRUCTIONS

1 For headboard, cut sticks into 1½-inch
lengths—approximately 10, or the
number needed to equal 1¼ inches
when placed side by side. Align the
sticks and hot-glue them together about
¼ inch from top and bottom. Wrap
twine around headboard to cover hot
glue at top.

2 Cut the following sticks:
- (2) sticks, 1¾ inches (bed side rails)
- (2) sticks, ⅞ inch (foot pieces)
- Stick, 1⅛ inches (between-feet piece)

3 Glue side rails to foot pieces, then side
rails to headboard. Glue 1⅛-inch piece
between foot pieces.

4 Wrap bedding around bed frame and
glue in place underneath.

rocket ship

3... 2... 1... blast off! Becoming an astronaut is something young ones often aspire to. Help them reach for the stars with this rocket ship!

creating the ship

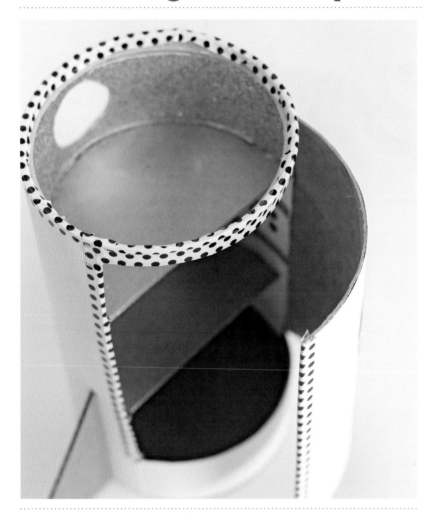

FINISHED SIZE

Approx. 16½-in. tall x 11-in. diameter (including fins)

MATERIALS + SUPPLIES

- Empty 42 oz. cylindrical oatmeal container, 9¾ x 5¼-in. diameter
- (3) sheets of white cardstock, 8 x 10 in.
- Sheet of one-sided glittered cardstock, 8 x 10 in.
- Corrugated cardboard, 5 x 7 in. (fins)
- Thin cardboard, 8 x 10 in. (inside floors)
- Thin white cardboard, 9¾ x 7¾ in. (wall reinforcement)
- Black and white striped scrapbook paper, 12 x 12 in. (nose cone)
- Black and white polka dotted washi tape, ¾-in. wide
- Black and white striped washi tape, ¾-in. wide
- Black and white print washi tape, ¾-in. wide
- Green and white striped washi tape, ¾-in. wide
- (2) paper stars, 1¼-in. square
- Red cardstock, 3 x 5 in.
- Yellow cardstock, 3 x 5 in.
- Dark blue cardstock, 3 x 5 in.
- ¼ in. paper punch
- ⅛ in. paper punch
- Craft knife
- Hot glue gun and glue sticks
- Scissors

creating the ship *(continued)*

Diagram 1

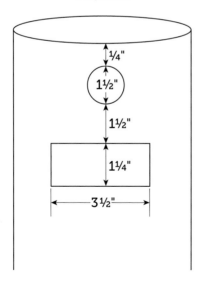

¼"

1½"

1½"

1¼"

3½"

INSTRUCTIONS

OUTSIDE

1 Set oatmeal lid aside. It will be used as the base of the nose cone.

2 For door, just below the plastic reinforcement ring around the top, draw a 5⅝-inch wide by 7½-inch tall rectangle on the container. Use a craft knife to cut along top, left side, and bottom, leaving the right vertical line uncut. On the inside, along the right side, score (but don't cut through) the vertical line from top to bottom to allow the door to open more easily.

3 Referring to diagram 1 for size and placement, cut the round and rectangular windows in the wall opposite the door.

4 Cover the outside of the container with white cardstock, using a separate piece for the door and cutting out the round and retangular window openings.

INSIDE

1 Place the wall reinforcement cardboard inside the container. Align the top and side edges with the container and press against the wall. From outside, draw the circle and retangular windows and cut them out. Glue the reinforcement to the walls.

2 Use diagram 2 (page 68) to cut two floor pieces from thin cardboard. Fold tabs down along dashed lines. Referring to photo, position one floor 2 inches below top plastic ring with tabs below the floor. Glue tabs to inside wall. Repeat with remaining floor 5½ inches below plastic ring.

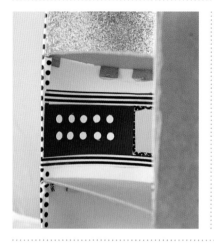

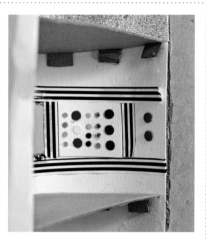

3 From glittered paper, cut a 9¾-inch long x 2-inch wide piece. Position it in the space above top floor. From outside, draw the round opening on paper; cut it out. Glue the rectangle to the wall. Glue the circle to the outside of the door.

4 Referring to photo, use paper punches to make circles from the glittered, white, red, blue, and yellow paper. For control panels on either side of rectangular window, place black and white striped washi tape.

FINISHING TOUCHES

1 Apply polka dotted washi tape around the top edge and along the door opening and door edge. Apply green and white striped washi tape around the round window and along door hinge. Apply black and white print washi tape around the opening of the rectangular window.

2 From corregated cardboard, use the diagram 3 fin pattern (page 68) to cut out three fins. Refer to photo for placement and glue in place. Glue stars to two side fins.

3 For nose cone, using black and white striped paper and lid as base, twist paper into a cone shape. Trim excess paper and align lid edge with bottom of cone so that cone is approximately 7¼-inches tall. Glue in place.

creating the ship (continued)

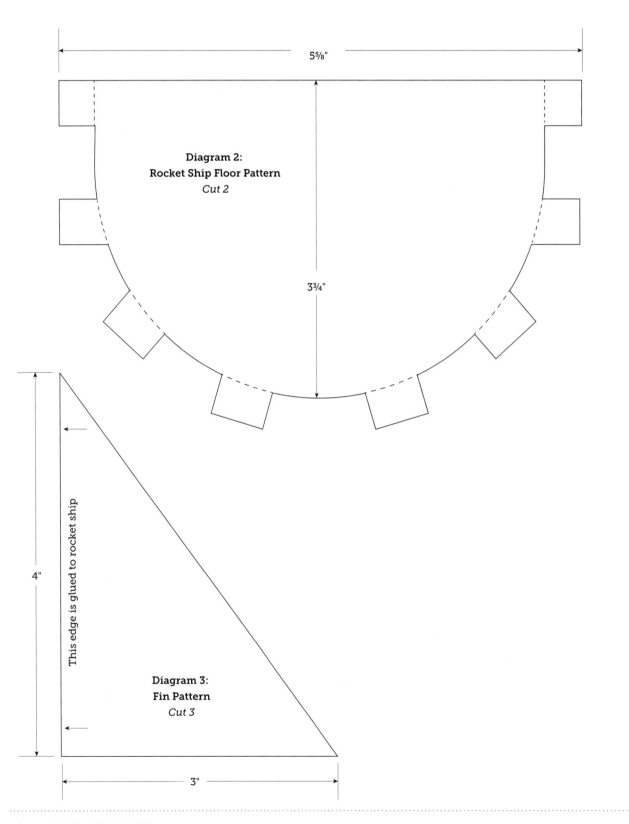

5⅝"

Diagram 2:
Rocket Ship Floor Pattern
Cut 2

3¾"

4"

This edge is glued to rocket ship

Diagram 3:
Fin Pattern
Cut 3

3"

about the designer

CHRISTEN BYRD

Christen Byrd loves all things creative—from graphic design to screenprinting to social/brand design to massive, custom balloon installations (more on that in a minute). She's the Creative Director for Loblolly Creamery, a local favorite in Little Rock, Arkansas. She's also the founder and head of Just Peachy, a balloon design company creating fun, over-the-top balloon installations for everything from corporate events to kids' parties and everything in between.

She and her husband Ryan have called Little Rock, Arkansas home for more than 10 years; it's where they raise their three children, Lucy, Olive, and Max, who are her biggest creative inspirations (they certainly served as the motivation for this book). As she developed each cardboard space, all three little Byrds were anxious to test them out and ask for new features. Christen's built-in focus group keeps her close to her audience and helped make this project a labor of love for her and her family.

about the writer

SUSAN WHITE SULLIVAN

Susan is best known for her long career in the craft publishing industry. The truth is that being the editorial director for a nationally known company allowed her to stay close to all the things she loved—sewing, crochet, knitting, painting, and more. It was the perfect mix of business and passion.

She formed her consulting firm in 2015 and continues to provide editorial services to the craft industry. In 2016, she authored her first sewing book, *Weighted Blankets, Vests & Scarves* (Spring House Press). Expanding her creative side, she is a contributor to craft magazines and teaches needle arts and mono printing at fiber festivals. She also teaches crochet and is past president of the Crochet Guild of America. She resides in Little Rock, Arkansas with her very patient husband.

metric conversions

In this book, I've used inches, yards, and ounces, showing anything less than one as a fraction. If you want to convert those to metric measurements, please use the following formulas:

FRACTIONS TO DECIMALS

⅛ = .125

¼ = .25

½ = .5

⅝ = .625

¾ = .75

IMPERIAL TO METRIC CONVERSION

LENGTH

Multiply inches by 25.4 to get millimeters

Multiply inches by 2.54 to get centimeters

Multiply yards by .9144 to get meters

For example, if you wanted to convert 1⅛ inches to millimeters:
1.125 in. x 25.4 mm = 28.575 mm

And to convert 2½ yards to meters:
2.5 yd. x .9144 m = 2.286 m

WEIGHT

Multiply ounces by 28.35 to get grams

Multiply pounds by .45 to get kilograms

For example, if you wanted to convert 5 ounces to grams:
5 oz. x 28.35 g = 141.75 g

And to convert 2 pounds to kilograms:
2 lb. x .45 kg = .9 kg

ALSO BY SUSAN WHITE SULLIVAN:

Weighted Blankets, Vests & Scarves

A weighted blanket is exactly what it sounds like—a blanket made heavy by the addition of polypropylene pellets sewn into the blanket itself. Weighted blankets—along with scarves and vests—are effective treatment for children and adults wrestling with the symptoms of anxiety, ADD/ADHD, autism spectrum disorder, PTSD, and other sensory disorders. Soft and warm, a weighted blanket is like a hug that relaxes the nervous system. *Weighted Blankets, Vests & Scarves* provides everything you need to make your own weighted blanket or garment. The easy-to-follow instructions and illustrations will guide you while the project photos will inspire you to craft a weighted blanket to soothe someone you love.

978-1-940611-46-4 | $12.99 | 48 Pages

index

Italic text signifies a project.

MORE GREAT BOOKS *from*
SPRING HOUSE PRESS

Fabulous Fat Quarter Aprons
978-1-940611-39-6
$12.99 | 56 Pages

Zippy Loom Creations
978-1-940611-79-2
$14.99 | 72 Pages

Afghan Loom Projects
978-1-940611-78-5
$16.99 | 72 Pages

Christmas Ornaments to Crochet
978-1-940611-48-8
$19.95 | 136 Pages

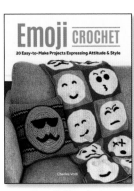

Emoji Crochet
978-1-940611-72-3
$19.95 | 128 Pages

Construction Vehicles to Crochet
978-1-940611-57-0
$22.95 | 128 Pages

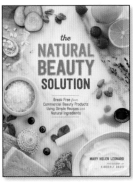

The Natural Beauty Solution
978-1-940611-18-1
$19.95 | 136 Pages

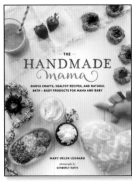

The Handmade Mama
978-1-940611-71-6
$27.95 | 200 Pages

String Art Magic
978-1-940611-73-0
$24.95 | 144 Pages

SPRING HOUSE PRESS

Look for these Spring House Press titles at your favorite bookstore, specialty retailer, or visit *www.springhousepress.com*.
For more information about Spring House Press, call 1-717-569-5196 or email us at *info@springhousepress.com*.